ANN ARBOR DISTRICT LIBRARY
31621211078420
WITHDRAWN

1943
BERLIN
THE SEVEN DWARVES
D1273903

CINEBOOK
EXPRESSO

Expresso Collection brings together stories published in one or two volumes by Cinebook. Single or double, you'll be able to savour the best European graphic novels selected for connoisseurs.

Other books in the same collection:

The Fascinating
Madame Tussaud
Follet - Duchâteau
ISBN 978-1-905460-36-6

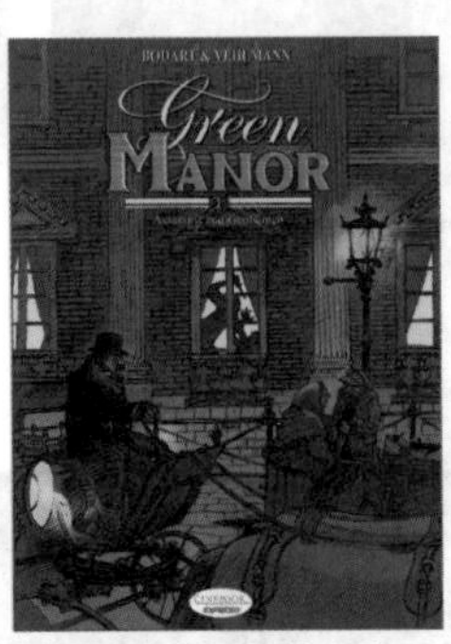

Green Manor Part 1
Assassins & Gentlemen
Bodart - Vehlmann
ISBN 978-1-905460-53-3

Green Manor Part 2
The Inconvenience
of Being Dead
Bodart - Vehlmann
ISBN 978-1-905460-64-9

Western
Rosinski - Van Hamme
ISBN 978-1-84918-084-9

Original title: Berlin – Les sept nains
Original edition: © Dargaud Benelux (Dargaud-Lombard S.A.), 2007 by Marvano
www.dargaud.com
All rights reserved
English translation: © 2012 Cinebook Ltd
Translator: Jerome Saincantin
Lettering and text layout: Imadjinn
Printed in Spain by Just Colour Graphic
This edition first published in Great Britain in 2012 by
Cinebook Ltd
56 Beech Avenue
Canterbury, Kent
CT4 7TA
www.cinebook.com
A CIP catalogue record for this book
is available from the British Library
ISBN 978-1-84918-135-8

PREFACE

WITHDRAWN

"NEVER IN THE FIELD OF HUMAN CONFLICT WAS SO MUCH OWED BY SO MANY TO SO FEW."
Winston Churchill

I will never forget. The shrill howling of air raid sirens. Dashing down the wooden stairs of that old building with no lift. The freezing cold cellar where the other tenants were already crammed. Waiting. My father explaining to me that it's the Allies who've come to bomb the bad Germans. The low rumbling of the approaching planes. Holding our breath. And sometimes—not always—the whistling of the bombs. My father was an atheist. So was I, of course, without knowing it. On those nights, though, I would pray. I would pray for the bombs to fall on others. Not on me. Not on us. I was scared. I was five. I was down below.

Above, too, they were scared. But I only learnt that later. British, Canadians, Poles, Americans, Belgians, Australians, French. They were between 18 and 22 years old. Most of them were too young to vote, to drive a car, to have a drink in a bar. But not too young to die aboard a 30-ton Lancaster with 2,000 gallons of fuel in the wings and six tons of bombs in the belly. Those kids were told they were men, soldiers; that they'd have to fight to save the free world. And they did. They were men. They did it. Pilots, gunners, navigators... Too many of those youth, their adolescence cut short, will never know their first wrinkle, their first grey hair—or even their first night of love. But they did it. With parched throats and insides knotted with fear, they did it. They saved the free world.

Mark Van Oppen, a.k.a. Marvano, was born in 1953. He never knew the war. He never heard the bombs whistling. And yet, he never forgot, either. His story, *The Seven Dwarves*, is probably one of the most moving, gripping and "real" that I've ever read in comic format. We're a long way here from Buck Danny, Tanguy, Dan Cooper and other paper heroes-who-always-win-in-the-end. Having done his research via several old RAF hands, Marvano virtually sat in the pilot's seat of the *S-Snowwhite* as it prepared to drop its thousands of pounds of death on Berlin and the Ruhr. He takes us through an almost cinematographic experience, what the seven crew members of the bomber—the seven dwarves of the title—lived through during their missions. Enemy fighters, flak, mid-air collisions, the fear, the need to piss, the temptation to drop their bombs just anywhere, an engine on fire, the rear gunner killed, the Lancaster at 10 o'clock exploding, the radio on the blink... And the return to base, too (when you're lucky enough to come back); counting the missing and trying to accept their loss with jaded resignation, the pleasures and the love you hurriedly latch onto, because you know that there might not be a tomorrow.

Mark Van Oppen isn't a friend. I've only met him once, briefly. What I'm writing here is not dictated by some bond of camaraderie, as often happens between members of the same brotherhood. My only intent is to share the emotion I felt when I read this story, masterfully built by an artist who, according to some persistent rumours in the world of comics, will soon become one of the truly great ones.

This briefing is over. Readers, to your aircraft!

Jean VAN HAMME

AUGUST 1993. LINCOLNSHIRE, ENGLAND.
DO YOU RECOGNISE ANYTHING?
A FEW THINGS. THE WINDMILL, YES... ALTHOUGH... IT SEEMS SMALLER THAN I RECALL...

BUT I NEVER CAME ALL THE WAY HERE. IT WAS A MILITARY ZONE.
TRUE. AND YET, YOU CAME IN ONCE. JUST ONCE.
WAS IT HERE THAT...?
I'M NOT ENTIRELY CERTAIN. IT'S BEEN 50 YEARS FOR ME, TOO.... BUT I THINK IT WAS HERE...

... THAT YOU GAVE HIM THIS.
...
OH, MY GOD!

2

BUT... HOW IS THAT POSSIBLE? WHY TODAY? WHY YOU? WHY DID YOU WAIT SO LONG TO...?

I DIDN'T KNOW YOU EXISTED. I... IT'S A LONG STORY. YOU SHOULD START BY READING THIS LETTER, EVEN THOUGH IT'S NOT REALLY ADDRESSED TO YOU.

19/8/1943
1943? BUT...
WAIT. READ IT FIRST.

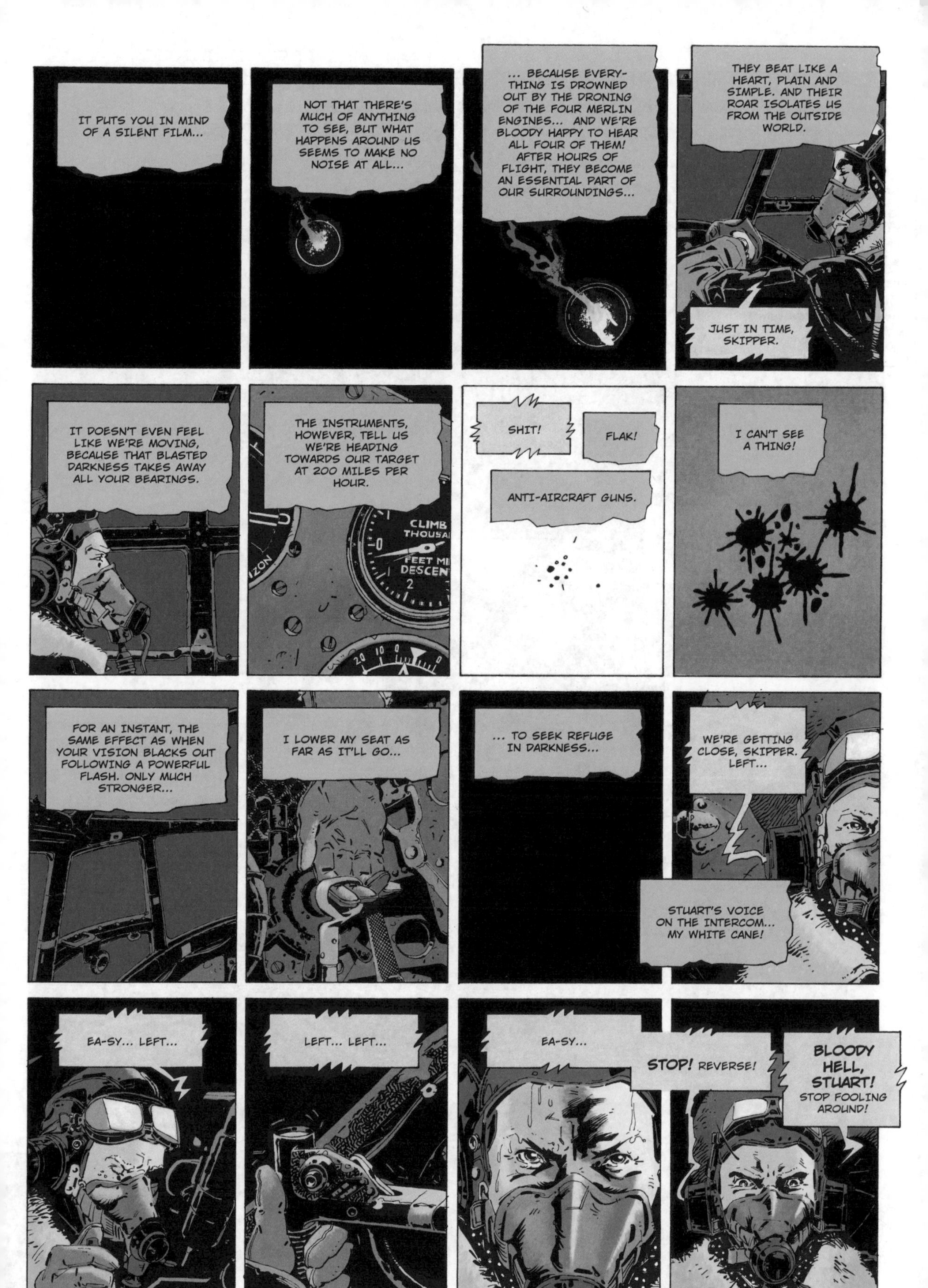

IT PUTS YOU IN MIND OF A SILENT FILM...
NOT THAT THERE'S MUCH OF ANYTHING TO SEE, BUT WHAT HAPPENS AROUND US SEEMS TO MAKE NO NOISE AT ALL...
... BECAUSE EVERYTHING IS DROWNED OUT BY THE DRONING OF THE FOUR MERLIN ENGINES... AND WE'RE BLOODY HAPPY TO HEAR ALL FOUR OF THEM! AFTER HOURS OF FLIGHT, THEY BECOME AN ESSENTIAL PART OF OUR SURROUNDINGS...
THEY BEAT LIKE A HEART, PLAIN AND SIMPLE. AND THEIR ROAR ISOLATES US FROM THE OUTSIDE WORLD.
JUST IN TIME, SKIPPER.
IT DOESN'T EVEN FEEL LIKE WE'RE MOVING, BECAUSE THAT BLASTED DARKNESS TAKES AWAY ALL YOUR BEARINGS.
THE INSTRUMENTS, HOWEVER, TELL US WE'RE HEADING TOWARDS OUR TARGET AT 200 MILES PER HOUR.
CLIMB
DESCENT
SHIT!
FLAK!
ANTI-AIRCRAFT GUNS.
I CAN'T SEE A THING!
FOR AN INSTANT, THE SAME EFFECT AS WHEN YOUR VISION BLACKS OUT FOLLOWING A POWERFUL FLASH. ONLY MUCH STRONGER...
I LOWER MY SEAT AS FAR AS IT'LL GO...
... TO SEEK REFUGE IN DARKNESS...
WE'RE GETTING CLOSE, SKIPPER. LEFT...
STUART'S VOICE ON THE INTERCOM... MY WHITE CANE!
EA-SY... LEFT...
LEFT... LEFT...
EA-SY...
STOP! REVERSE!
BLOODY HELL, STUART! STOP FOOLING AROUND!

JUST JOKING, SKIPPER. BOMBS GONE!
THE LANCASTER BUCKS UP WHEN THE SIX TONS OF BOMBS ARE DROPPED.
WITH THE BOMB BAY CLOSED, WE PUT THE NOSE DOWN TO GAIN SOME SPEED AND BANK LEFT SHARPLY...
LET'S BUGGER OFF, AUBIE! IT'S GETTING TOO HOT HERE!
YOU SAID IT.
FOR A MOMENT, I CAN SEE WHAT'S GOING ON BELOW. THE RUHR... WE CALL IT "HAPPY VALLEY..."
HAPPY VALLEY! SOMETIMES I WONDER WHAT MORON CAME UP WITH THAT NICKNAME!
SOUNDS LIKE TYPICAL OFFICER HUMOUR TO ME. AM I RIGHT, STUART?
4.

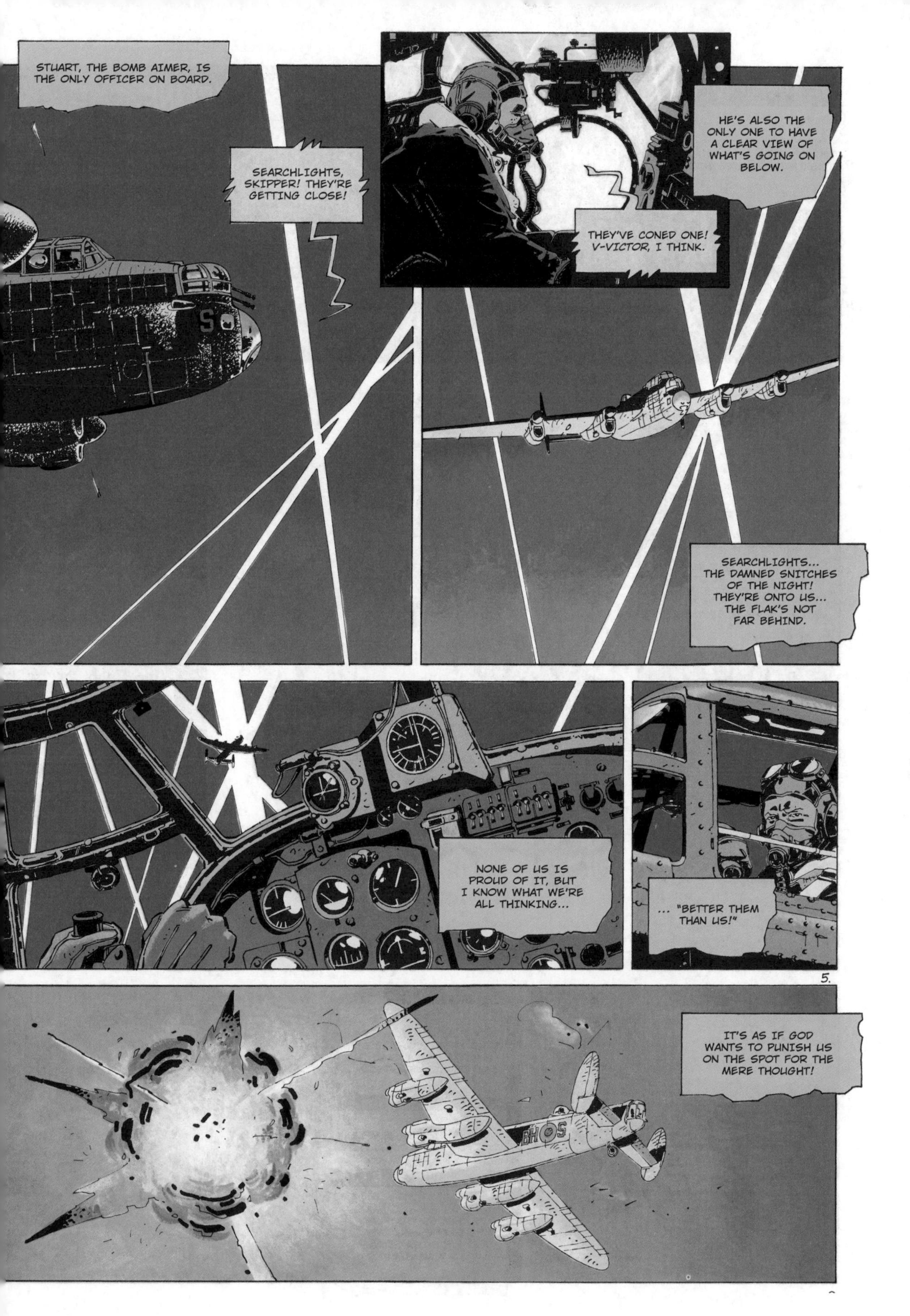
STUART, THE BOMB AIMER, IS THE ONLY OFFICER ON BOARD.
HE'S ALSO THE ONLY ONE TO HAVE A CLEAR VIEW OF WHAT'S GOING ON BELOW.
SEARCHLIGHTS, SKIPPER! THEY'RE GETTING CLOSE!
THEY'VE CONED ONE! V-VICTOR, I THINK.
SEARCHLIGHTS... THE DAMNED SNITCHES OF THE NIGHT! THEY'RE ONTO US... THE FLAK'S NOT FAR BEHIND.
NONE OF US IS PROUD OF IT, BUT I KNOW WHAT WE'RE ALL THINKING...
... "BETTER THEM THAN US!"
5.
IT'S AS IF GOD WANTS TO PUNISH US ON THE SPOT FOR THE MERE THOUGHT!
BH S

NOT OUR TIME YET. THEY'RE AFTER V-VICTOR. NOT US. NOT S-SNOWWHITE.
PLINK
PLINK
PLINK
PLINK
PLINK
PLINK
PLINK PLINK
PLINK
PLINK
PLINK
PLINK
PLINK
PLINK PLINK
PLINK
THAT'S ANOTHER THING YOU CAN HEAR WHEN A SHELL BURSTS CLOSE ENOUGH: THE SOUND OF SHRAPNEL HITTING THE FUSELAGE...

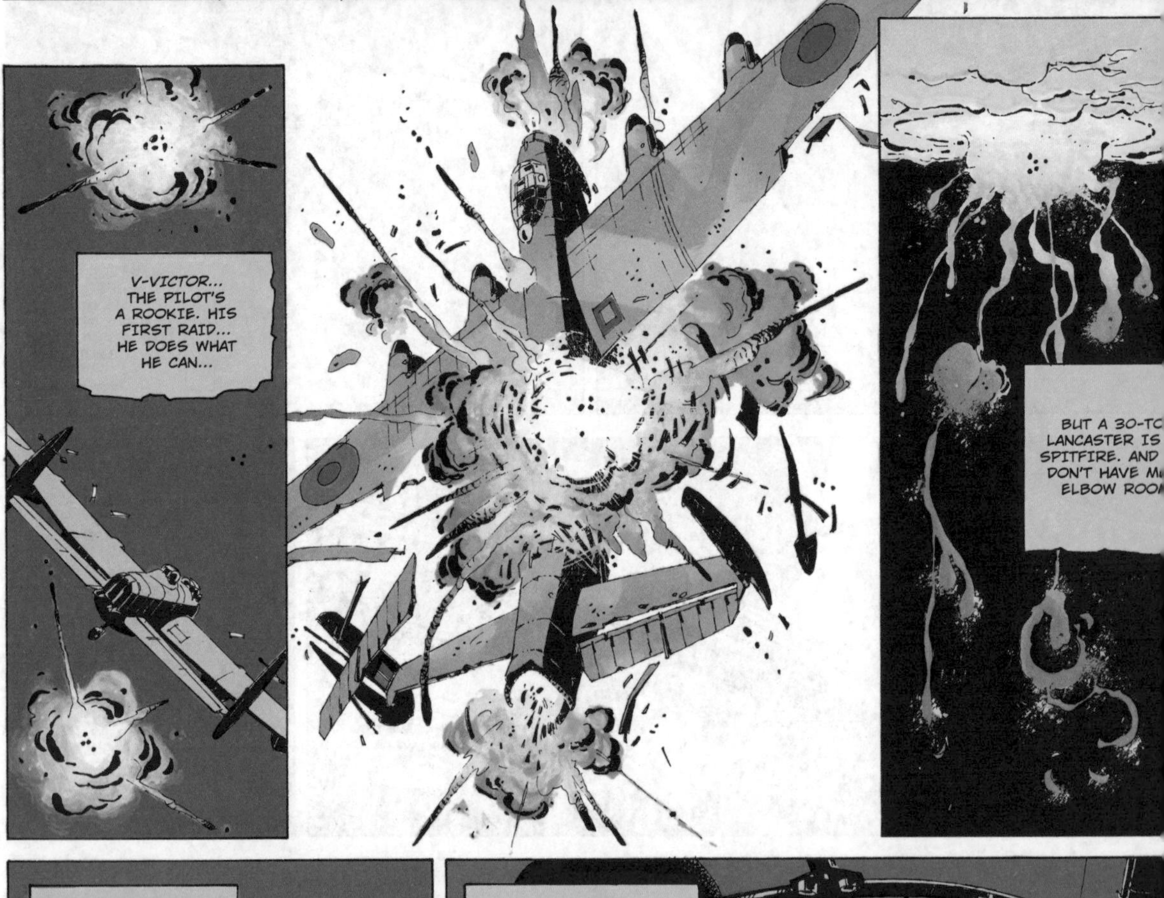

V-VICTOR... THE PILOT'S A ROOKIE. HIS FIRST RAID... HE DOES WHAT HE CAN...
BUT A 30-TC LANCASTER IS SPITFIRE. AND DON'T HAVE M ELBOW ROO

EVEN IF YOU CAN'T SEE THEM, THEY'RE THERE.
SIX HUNDRED BOMBERS LIKE S-SNOWWHITE. SIX HUNDRED "HEAVIES" IN ONE TIGHT FORMATION...
THE CHOICE IS SIMPLE: THE FLAK OR A COLLISION.
I CHOOSE THE FLAK. I STAY ON COURSE AND KEEP THE HICCUPS TO A MINIMUM.

I TRY TO CLIMB AS HIGH AS POSSIBLE...
... UNTIL ALL IS DARK AROUND ME.
ONLY OWLS AND FOOLS FLY AT NIGHT.
THE FLAK SLACKENS. THE TERROR REMAINS. IT BEGINS WITH A FAINT LIGHT TO PORT...
AND IT KEEPS ON GROWING. WE ALL KNOW WHAT IT IS...
... AND WHAT IT MUST MEAN.
FIGHTERS! CHECK FOR BANDITS! BIRDWATCH! BIRDWATCH!
IT'S AN EXPRESSION COINED BY NELSON, THE WIRELESS OPERATOR. AN AMATEUR ORNITHOLOGIST...
OUR LIFE DEPENDS ON WHO SEES WHOM FIRST. THE TURRETS TURN BACK AND FORTH, BACK AND FORTH...
PILOT TO NAVIGATOR. COLIN, JOIN THE LOOK-OUT. I'LL CALL YOU IF WE GET LOST...
EASY AS PIE, SKIPPER. TURN LEFT AT THE CROSSROADS.

*NICKNAME OF THE WIRELESS OPERATOR

THOSE WITH THE GOOD FORTUNE TO HAVE ENOUGH FUEL LEFT ARE DIVERTED TOWARDS SOUTHERN AIRFIELDS.
FOG IS EVEN WORSE THAN DARKNESS. YOU CAN'T SEE THE RUNWAY APPROACH LIGHTS.
WE'RE GONNA HANG OUT THE WASHING ON THE SIEGFRIED LINE, 'CAUSE THE WASHING DAY IS HERE
ANDING IN A BOWL OF PEA OUP. THAT'S WHAT IT BOILS OWN TO. THAT'S HOW FOUR LANCASTERS CRASHED ON ANDING LAST WEEK. THERE WAS ONE FATALITY.
AN ONLOOKER.
A MESS SERGEANT. A PROPELLER FROM A LANC THAT HAD MISSED THE RUNWAY TOOK OFF HIS HEAD.
IN A WAY, THE PILOT DIDN'T SURVIVE EITHER. HE HAD TO BE PUT OUT TO PASTURE AMONG GROUND PERSONNEL. FOR "LACK OF MORAL FIBRE," IN OFFICIAL RAF PARLANCE.
WHAT DOES MORAL FIBRE HAVE TO DO WITH ANYTHING?
REAR AIR GUNNER TO PILOT! AUBIE, I HAVE TO TAKE A LEAK!
9.
SORRY, NIGEL. I FORGOT. GO AHEAD.
CONTROL TOWER TO ALL BOMBERS! WARNING! DARKY! DARKY!
CAN'T EVEN HAVE A CUPPA IN PEACE!
DARKY... A STRAY BOMBER. PROBABLY WITHOUT WIRELESS. MAYBE EVEN WITHOUT INSTRUMENTS.
AHHHH! FINALLY!

BLOODY HELL!
HEY?!
AUBIE!
WE'RE GONNA HANG OUT THE WASHING ON THE SIEGFRIED LINE
10.
S-SNOWWHITE TO TOWER. MAYDAY! MAYDAY! COLLISION WITH DARKY!

PILOT TO CREW. OK, WE CAN KEEP IT IN THE AIR. INTERCOM CHECK.
BOMB AIMER TO PILOT. I'M ALL RIGHT.
NAVIGATOR OK, AUBIE.
FLIGHT ENGINEER OK. DARKY'S GOING DOWN.
SPARKS HERE. ALL GOOD, SKIPPER.
MID-UPPER GUNNER, CHECK.
REAR AIR GUNNER?
REAR AIR GUNNER?! NIGEL, WHERE ARE YOU?
NIGEL!
ALAN, GET BACK THERE AND...
HEADING TO THE REAR, SKIPPER!
NIGE'S OK!
JUST A BIT SHAKEN.
IF THE SIEGFRIED LINE'S STILL THERE
S-SNOWWHITE TO TOWER. REAR TURRET AND PORT TAIL ARE GONE. I'M BRINGING THIS CRATE IN—NOW!
WE USE THE BURNING WRECK OF THE DARKY AS A BEACON. LANDING'S NO LONGER A PROBLEM.
11

UNTIL YOUR EYES GET USED TO THE DARKNESS, TAKE IT EASY!
AS USUAL, THE DEBRIEFING DOES US IN. THEY SERVE US TEA WITH RUM.
BLAST IT, AUBERSON! COULDN'T YOU BE A TAD MORE SPECIFIC THAN JUST "FLAK SOMEWHERE AROUND BREMEN...?"
SWEETHEART, TO BE HONEST I'M GLAD I'M ABLE TO TELL THAT MUCH.
I HATE RUM.
I GIVE NIGEL MY RATION. HE'S STILL A LITTLE PALE...
AND HE WON'T LET GO OF YVETTE, OUR MASCOT.
OH, ISN'T HE THE CUTEST OF MUMMIES!
THROW IT AWAY, NIGE! I'LL MAKE YOU ANOTHER ONE!
A GOOD THING YOUR MOTHER CAN'T HEAR YOU, WALKER. SHE'D GIVE YOU SUCH A SPANKING...
BY THE TIME WE'RE FINALLY ALLOWED TO GO TO BED, HE'S FEELING PERFECTLY FINE.
ON HER... HIC!... LOVELY LIPS!
HE'S SHOT TO RIBBONS!
I'M NOT SURPRISED. HE'S DOWNED THE RUM RATIONS FROM THREE CREWS!
NO SMOKING
IT'S A GREAT DAY! Watch some bastard spoil it!
SWITCH OFF ENGINE
PETROL
WHEN WE WAKE UP, THERE ARE THOSE EMPTY BUNKS... THE KITS TO SORT OUT...
... AND THE PERSONAL LOCKERS THAT MUST BE BROKEN INTO. SOME CHAPS REFUSE TO HAND OVER THEIR KEYS BEFORE GOING ON OPERATION.
MP
12.

EY'RE RIGHT. NO
D TO TEMPT FATE.
GO ON, SARAH. JUST GIVE IN. WE'RE GOING TO THE GREY HORSE WITH BOB AND FRED.
NO, REALLY. I'M BEAT. I WAS ON DUTY FOR A FULL DAY AND NIGHT. KAREN WAS SICK, AND...
W.A.A.F. OUT OF BOUNDS TO R.A.F. WITHIN 25 FEET OF THIS NOTICE
BARNEY? YUMMY SICKNESS!
YOU THINK SO? BARNEY'S MARRIED.
HOW DO YOU KNOW?
EASY: I SORT THE MAIL.
YOU SHOULD TELL HER, THEN.
I DID. SHE SAYS SHE DOESN'T CARE. SHE JUST WANTS TO HAVE SOME FUN.
HUT 7 W.A.A.F.
HEY! THERE'S SOMEONE KNOCKING AT THE DOOR, GIRLS!
SERGEANT AUBERSON! THIS AREA IS OFF LIMITS TO MEN! CAN'T YOU READ?
NO, I'M THE RESIDENT ILLITERATE DEAF-MUTE. HELLO, MAUREEN.
HUT 7 W.A.A.F.
W.A.A.F. OUT OF BOUNDS TO R.A.F. WITHIN 25 FEET OF THIS NOTICE
SO, THAT'S WHY YOU DIDN'T WANT TO COME WITH US TO THE GREY HORSE!
SARAH! IT'S FOR YOU–ALAS!
AUBIE, DARLING!
LADIES, LADIES, PLEASE...
!...
13.
HELLO, AUBIE.
GOOD EVENING. I... I JUST...
AHEM!

WELL, WE'RE OFF, THEN!
MAKE YOURSELF AT HOME, AUBIE. MY BED'S YOURS.
SARAH, IF YOU DON'T WANT TO BE DISTURBED, JUST PUT A HANDKERCHIEF IN THE WINDOW...

NOW, GIRLS...
HEEHEE HEE!

SORRY ABOUT THAT. THEY'RE TERRIBLE...

I FORGOT. I HAVE SOMETHING FOR YOU...

OH, AUBIE.

THANK YOU. YOU'RE A DARLING.

SARAH, I...

NO, AUBIE. DON'T SAY IT.

I COULDN'T. IT'S TOO SOON.

don't be like
HALF TRAINED HARRY
"THAT ONE'S NOT COMING THIS WAY..."
FAMOUS LAST WORDS
BESIDES, HE MUST HAVE MANAGED TO BAIL OUT. HE COULD BE A PRISONER OF WAR.

IT'S POSSIBLE, ISN'T IT?

YES, OF COURSE.
OF COURSE IT'S POSSIBLE.

BESIDES, I'M TOO OLD FOR YOU. I'M 24, AND YOU'RE ONLY 19.

ALMOST 20. NO NEED TO EXAGGERATE.

YOU CAN FIND YOURSELF A YOUNGER GIRLFRIEND. YOU PROBABLY HAVE ONE ALREADY.
I DON'T HAVE ANY GIRLFRIENDS.
ASIDE FROM YVETTE.
YVETTE? WHO'S YVETTE? DO YOU LOVE HER?
B

YVETTE'S S-SNOWWHITE'S MASCOT. THE OLD SKIPPER GAVE HER TO ME.

SHE'S GOOD LUCK. YES, I LOVE HER.
THANKS.

YOU SMOKE TOO MUCH, AUBIE.
I KNOW. CHEERS!
CHEERS!

15.

TELL ME, THIS HIRT... WHY ARE OU CARRYING IT WITH YOU?

ER...
WELL...

IT'S TORN, AND I THOUGHT...
YOU THOUGHT THAT MAYBE I HAD SOME NEEDLES AND THREAD? I DO, YES.

I'LL GIVE THEM TO YOU AND TEACH YOU HOW TO MEND A SHIRT.
ME?!
BUT...
WHEN THE LIGHTS GO ON AGAIN ALL OVER THE WORLD...
NOW GIVE IT A SHARP PULL. THERE. DO YOU HAVE A RAID TONIGHT?
NO. THE REAR TURRET ON S-SNOWWHITE HAS TO BE REPLACED.
OW!
I THINK I'LL GO TO THE FARM NEAR THE BASE TOMORROW. THE FARMERS ARE SHORT-HANDED.
THAT'S A GOOD IDEA.
AND THE BOYS ARE HOME AGAIN ALL OVER THE WORLD...
AND RAIN OR SNOW IS ALL THAT MAY FALL FROM THE SKIES ABOVE...
A KISS WON'T MEAN GOODBYE...
COME NOW, AUBIE! YOU COULD SPOT THOSE STITCHES OF YOURS FROM 50 FEET AWAY!
HEY, HOW ABOUT YOU SHOW ME HOW WELL YOU CAN FLY A BOMBER, HUH?
BUT A LOAN TO LOVE.
ROOOOOO

THEY'RE MEAN!

WHO'S MEAN?
THE PLANES.
OH!
MY NAME'S DAVID. WHAT'S YOURS?

LISA.
BUT, THAT'S ME?!
OF COURSE IT IS.
WHAT ABOUT YOUR DOLL? WHAT'S HER NAME?
SNOW WHITE.

WHAT A COINCIDENCE! THAT'S ALSO MY PLANE'S NAME.
SNOW WHITE?
YES.
WHY?
HMM... BECAUSE IT'S ALL BLACK, I THINK. AND BECAUSE THERE ARE SEVEN OF US FLYING IN IT... LIKE THE SEVEN DWARVES.

BUT SNOW WHITE ISN'T BLACK.
NO, BUT SHE'S GOT BLACK HAIR.
THAT'S TRUE.
I HAVE A DOLL TOO.

YOU? A DOLL?
YES. I ALWAYS TAKE HER WITH ME WHEN I FLY SNOWWHITE.
AND YOU PLAY WITH HER?

PLAY? NO. I JUST TAKE HER ALONG, THAT'S ALL. THE TRUTH IS, SHE'S NOT REALLY MINE. SHE BELONGS TO ALL SEVEN OF US. OR TO THE PLANE. WE THINK SHE PROTECTS OUR PLANE.

COULD I SEE HER?
I DON'T HAVE HER HERE WITH ME. BUT, OF COURSE YOU CAN SEE HER. I'LL...
WHAT ARE YOU DOING HERE, FLIGHT SERGEANT?

I... MY BOMBER IS UNDER REPAIR AT THE BASE NEAR HERE...
I THOUGHT I MIGHT GIVE YOU A HAND WITH THE HARVEST...

18.

I'M NOT IN CHARGE HERE, FLIGHT SERGEANT. THE MAN COMING NOW IS. BUT WE DON'T NEED ANY HELP.
WE'RE DOING ABSOLUTELY FINE.
DAD! THE GENTLEMAN, DAVID, HE'S GOT A PLANE CALLED SNOW WHITE, AND A DOLL, AND...
JOE, WHO'S THE LAD?
FLIGHT SERGEANT DAVID AUBERSON, SIR. I CAME TO SEE IF YOU MIGHT NEED SOME HELP.
SURE, LADDIE, SURE. DO YOU KNOW HOW TO LEAD HORSES?
I'VE NEVER TRIED, SIR. BUT I DO LOVE HORSES.
WELL, THAT'S SETTLED, THEN. MY NAME'S CRAYDON, TREVOR CRAYDON, AND THIS IS...
I'M TAKING LISA BACK TO THE FARM, CRAYDON.
I HAVE TO REST MY LEG.
!
OF COURSE, JOE. AS YOU WISH.
DAVID, WHEN CAN I SEE YOUR DOLL?
I'LL BRING HER NEXT TIME, LISA. I PROMISE.
19.
COME ON, LAD.
LET'S GET TO WORK.

WE HAVE TO FLY 30 RAIDS IN ORDER TO COMPLETE OUR TOUR OF OPERATIONS.
ALAN HAS ADDED A BOMB ONTO S-SNOWWHITE'S NOSE. THE 24TH. SEVENTEEN OF THEM OURS.
NOT BAD. THE AVERAGE IS ABOUT 11...
WHAT'S THIS, THEN? DOESN'T STUART USUALLY TAKE CARE OF THE PAINT JOB?
YOU'RE NOT GOING TO BELIEVE THIS, SKIPPER, BUT HE'S IN BED WITH A TEMPERATURE OF 104.

HERMANN GÖRING ONCE SAID: "NO ENEMY BOMBER CAN REACH THE RUHR. IF ONE REACHES THE RUHR, MY NAME IS NOT GÖRING. YOU MAY CALL ME MEYER."
THAT'S WHAT PEOPLE FROM THE RUHR AND BERLIN HAVE BEEN CALLING HIM FOR A LONG TIME...
HIHO! HIHO! IT'S OFF TO WORK WE G

BERLIN... IT'LL BE BERLIN TONIGHT, I'M AFRAID. BRIEFINGS AREN'T UNTIL THE EVENINGS, BUT AN EXPERIENCED PILOT ONLY NEEDS A FEW CLUES...
HEY, JONESY! HOW MUCH ARE WE GETTING TO DRINK?

FULL TANK FOR ALL, AUBIE!

"FULL TANK..." THAT'S 2,154 GALLONS. A LONG-RANGE FLIGHT. PROBABLY BERLIN...

A LANCASTER'S FUEL TANKS ARE LOCATED IN THE WINGS. GERMAN FIGHTERS KNOW IT ALL TOO WELL. THE WINGS ARE ONE OF THEIR FAVOURITE TARGETS. AND THERE'S PLENTY TO AIM FOR! ABOUT 100 FEET...
BH

THIS TIME, THE BOMB LOAD DOESN'T TELL US MUCH. TWELVE 500-POUND BOMBS AND A TWO-TON "COOKIE"—TNT AND AMMONIUM NITRATE. IT'S ONLY WHEN THEY BRING AN ADDITIONAL LOAD OF INCENDIARIES THAT WE START TO GET AN IDEA OF THE TARGET...
... A CITY MADE UP MOSTLY OF WOODEN HOUSES...

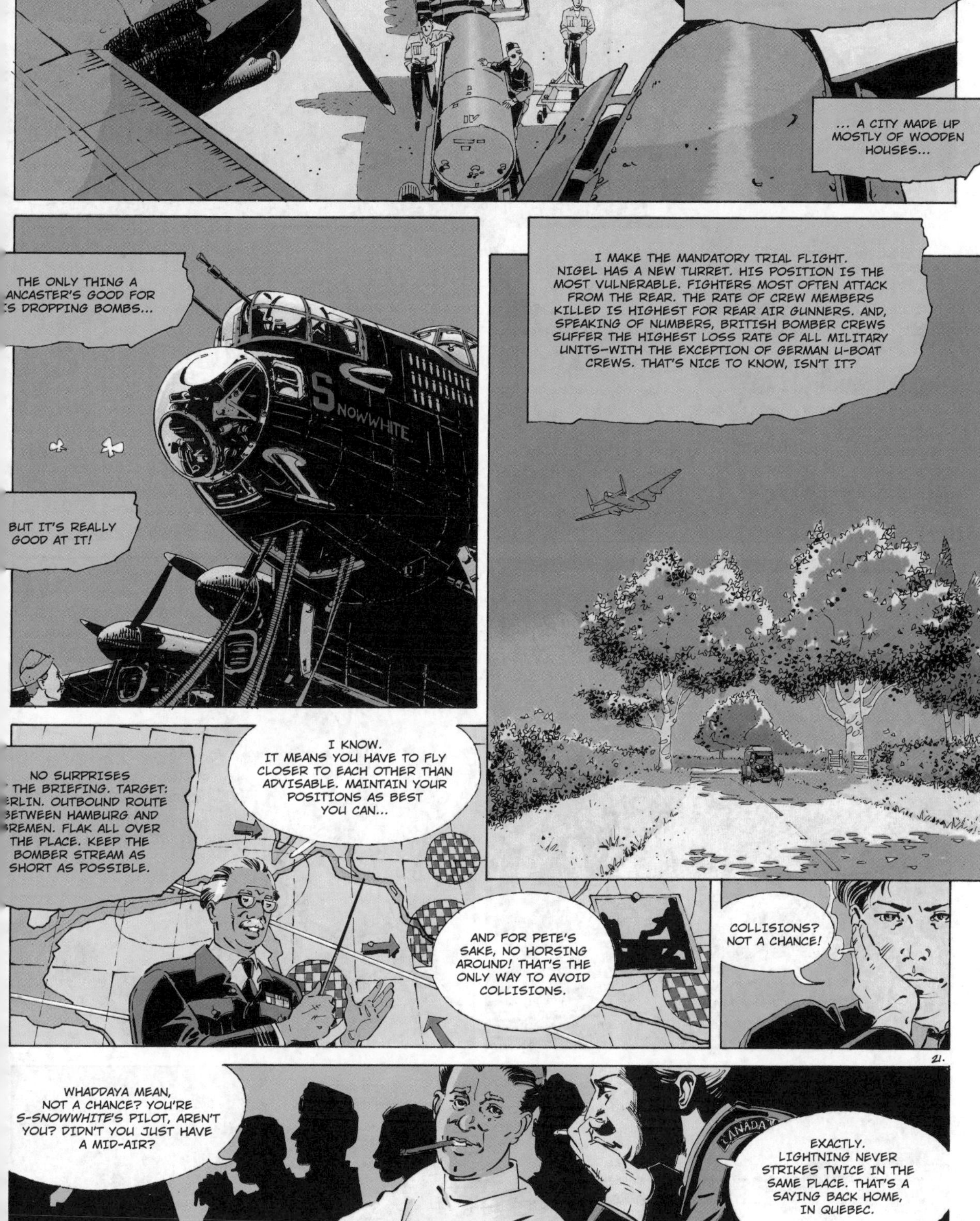
THE ONLY THING A ANCASTER'S GOOD FOR 'S DROPPING BOMBS...
SNOWWHITE
BUT IT'S REALLY GOOD AT IT!
I MAKE THE MANDATORY TRIAL FLIGHT. NIGEL HAS A NEW TURRET. HIS POSITION IS THE MOST VULNERABLE. FIGHTERS MOST OFTEN ATTACK FROM THE REAR. THE RATE OF CREW MEMBERS KILLED IS HIGHEST FOR REAR AIR GUNNERS. AND, SPEAKING OF NUMBERS, BRITISH BOMBER CREWS SUFFER THE HIGHEST LOSS RATE OF ALL MILITARY UNITS—WITH THE EXCEPTION OF GERMAN U-BOAT CREWS. THAT'S NICE TO KNOW, ISN'T IT?
NO SURPRISES THE BRIEFING. TARGET: ERLIN. OUTBOUND ROUTE BETWEEN HAMBURG AND REMEN. FLAK ALL OVER THE PLACE. KEEP THE BOMBER STREAM AS SHORT AS POSSIBLE.
I KNOW. IT MEANS YOU HAVE TO FLY CLOSER TO EACH OTHER THAN ADVISABLE. MAINTAIN YOUR POSITIONS AS BEST YOU CAN...
AND FOR PETE'S SAKE, NO HORSING AROUND! THAT'S THE ONLY WAY TO AVOID COLLISIONS.
COLLISIONS? NOT A CHANCE!
21.

WHADDAYA MEAN, NOT A CHANCE? YOU'RE S-SNOWWHITE'S PILOT, AREN'T YOU? DIDN'T YOU JUST HAVE A MID-AIR?
EXACTLY. LIGHTNING NEVER STRIKES TWICE IN THE SAME PLACE. THAT'S A SAYING BACK HOME, IN QUEBEC.
CANADA

THAT'S WHAT THEY SAY BACK HOME IN THE STATES, TOO, BUDDY. BUT LET ME TELL YOU THIS: IF ANYTHING CAN GO WRONG, YOU CAN BET YOUR ASS IT WILL GO WRONG. IT'S A LAW, AUBERSON.
ANOTHER LAW FOR YOU: SOME OF THE CHAPS HERE WON'T BE COMING BACK. IN OUR GROUP ALONE, 60 CRATES LOST OVER THE LAST MONTH...
BY THE WAY, THE NAME'S MURPHY. I VOLUNTEERED RIGHT FROM THE START–EVEN BEFORE THE JAPS ATTACKED PEARL HARBOR.
SIXTY TIMES SEVEN. YOU DO THE MATH.
LAY OFF THE IDEALISM, MURPHY. WE'RE ALL VOLUNTEERS. EVEN THE BRITISH.
MOST OF US ARE TOO YOUNG TO VOTE... OR TO DRIVE A CAR.
DORNIER DO 217 NIGHT FIGHTER
BUT NOT TOO YOUNG TO GO BOMB JERRY IN A 30-TON, FOUR-ENGINE KITE. AND NOT TOO YOUNG TO DIE... WHEN WE GO PICK UP OUR PARACHUTES, WE ALWAYS TELL THE SAME STUPID JOKES...
H
IF IT DOESN'T OPEN, I'LL RETURN IT, SWEETHEART!

IF A CHAP'S BAILED OUT BEFORE, HE BELONGS TO THE "CATERPILLAR CLUB"–SO CALLED BECAUSE THE PARACHUTES ARE MADE OF SILK. I HEAR THE AMERICANS USE A DIFFERENT FABRIC–NYLON, OR SOMETHING LIKE THAT. PEOPLE IN OCCUPIED COUNTRIES, THEY'D MUCH RATHER SEE A BRIT FALL FROM THE SKY THAN A YANK. EASILY UNDERSTANDABLE! I DON'T SEE THEM MAKING ANY CLOTHES WITH THAT NYLON OF THEIRS! OR STOCKINGS! THE SILK STOCKINGS WE'RE ISSUED ARE ABSOLUTELY VITAL. IF MY FEET FREEZE, I WON'T BE ABLE TO PUSH THE RUDDER PEDALS...

AND THE HEATING ON A LANC ISN'T WORTH A PENNY. MINUS 20 IS COMMON UP THERE.
WHAT DO YOU HAVE AGAINST IDEALISM, AUBERSON? DAMMIT, I'D RATHER DIE FOR AN IDEAL, FOR A GOOD CAUSE.
OH!
CPL PATINKIN
22

I'D RATHER NOT DIE AT ALL!

STIFF UPPER LIP, NIGEL! THERE'S A W.A.A.F. AT THE WHEEL!
GOD SAVE US!
WE'RE DRIVEN TO THE AIRCRAFT...
NO NEED TO LUG ALL YOUR KIT, BOYS. I'LL BRING IT TO YOUR KITE IN A MINUTE.
YOU'RE A DARLING, CORPORAL.
DOING ANYTHING IN THE MORNING?
AH, THE PRIVILEGES OF GLADIATORS...
TO REPLACE STUART (18 OPS, 104° FEVER), WE'VE BEEN GIVEN A SPROG (18 YEARS OLD, NOWHERE NEAR 104 HOURS OF FLIGHT SINCE COMING OUT OF TRAINING). WE HAVE ALL SEVEN DWARVES AGAIN. EVERY CREW HAS ITS OWN RITUALS BEFORE TAKEOFF.
23

WE ALWAYS TAKE A LEAK AGAINST THE TAIL WHEEL.
HI 296

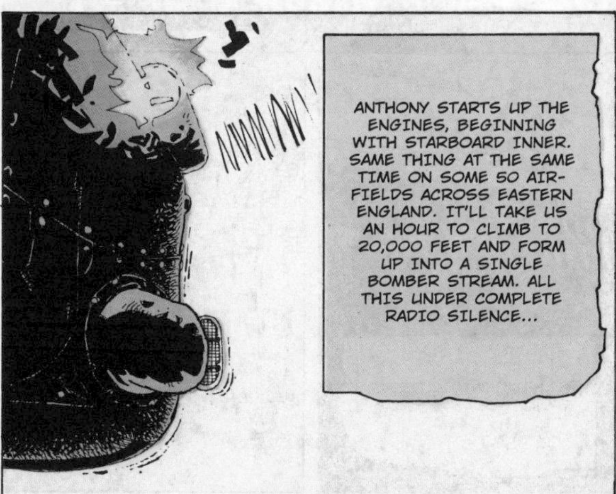
NNNNW!
ANTHONY STARTS UP THE ENGINES, BEGINNING WITH STARBOARD INNER. SAME THING AT THE SAME TIME ON SOME 50 AIRFIELDS ACROSS EASTERN ENGLAND. IT'LL TAKE US AN HOUR TO CLIMB TO 20,000 FEET AND FORM UP INTO A SINGLE BOMBER STREAM. ALL THIS UNDER COMPLETE RADIO SILENCE...

TAXIING IN A LANCASTER IS A ROTTEN JOB. THE PERIMETER TRACK'S 50 FEET WIDE AND YOU CAN'T REALLY PROPERLY STEER ANYTHING. ALL YOU CAN DO IS WORK THE REVS OF THE OUTER ENGINES AND USE THE BRAKES. IF ONE OF THE WHEELS GOES OFF THE TRACK, THE LANC WILL BOG DOWN IN THE GRASS LIKE A LUMP AND BLOCK THE PLANES BEHIND IT. ONE STUPID INCIDENT LIKE THAT CAN SCRAP A WHOLE RAID.
HEY, NELSON, YOU'RE SWISS, RIGHT? LISTEN...
I'M NOT SWISS! MY MOTHER'S SWISS, NOT ME!
BH S
OH, RIGHT. ANYWAY, LISTEN. AFTER A RAID ON REGENSBURG, THIS B-17 FINDS HIMSELF OVER SWITZERLAND...
OH, FOR PETE'S SAKE! SKIPPER, TURN OFF THE INTERCOM! ALAN'S TRYING TO TELL A SWISS JOKE!
WAIT, AUBIE, IT'S A GOOD ONE! SO, THIS B-17 IS TOOLING ALONG OVER SWITZERLAND WHEN SWISS AIR CONTROL GOES AND CALLS HIM.
"YOU ARE VIOLATING THE AIRSPACE OF A NEUTRAL COUNTRY," SAYS THE SWISS. "I KNOW," ANSWERS THE SKIPPER OF THE B-17.
WE GET THE GREEN LIGHT...
24
THE SWISS CONTROLLER: "IF YOU DON'T LAND IMMEDIATELY, WE WILL OPEN FIRE." "I KNOW," THE SKIPPER TELLS HIM, AND BLITHELY KEEPS FLYING ON.
!
HIHO! HIHO! IT'S OFF TO WORK WE GO!
AS USUAL, WE'RE BEING WAVED GOODBYE FROM THE BASE.

SUDDENLY HE SEES A SHELL BURST ABOUT 20 MILES AWAY. "HEY, BUDDY," SAYS THE SKIPPER TO THE SWISS. "YOU DON'T SHOOT TOO STRAIGHT!"
AND THE SWISS DRILY ANSWERS: "I KNOW!"
SO?
IT'S A GOOD ONE, ISN'T IT?
WISH ME LUCK AS YOU WAVE ME GOODBYE
VERY GOOD, ALAN. SO FUNNY I MIGHT PUKE!
CHEERIO, HERE I GO, ON MY WAY
WISH ME LUCK AS YOU WAVE ME GOODBYE WITH A CHEER, NOT A TEAR, MAKE IT GAY
HMPH... NO SENSE OF HUMOUR, THESE SWISS!
GIVE ME A SMILE I CAN KEEP ALL THE WHILE IN MY HEART WHILE I'M AWAY
'TILL WE MEET ONCE AGAIN YOU AND I
25
PIN
WISH ME LUCK AS YOU WAVE ME GOODBYE
TWO HUNDRED AND TEN MILES PER HOUR. COURSE 090 MAGNETIC.
NAVIGATOR HERE. ENEMY COAST DEAD AHEAD, SKIPPER.
ROGER THAT, COLIN. CAN YOU LET ME KNOW WHEN JERRY PICKS US UP ON RADAR?
EASY-PEASY, SKIPPER: HE HAS!

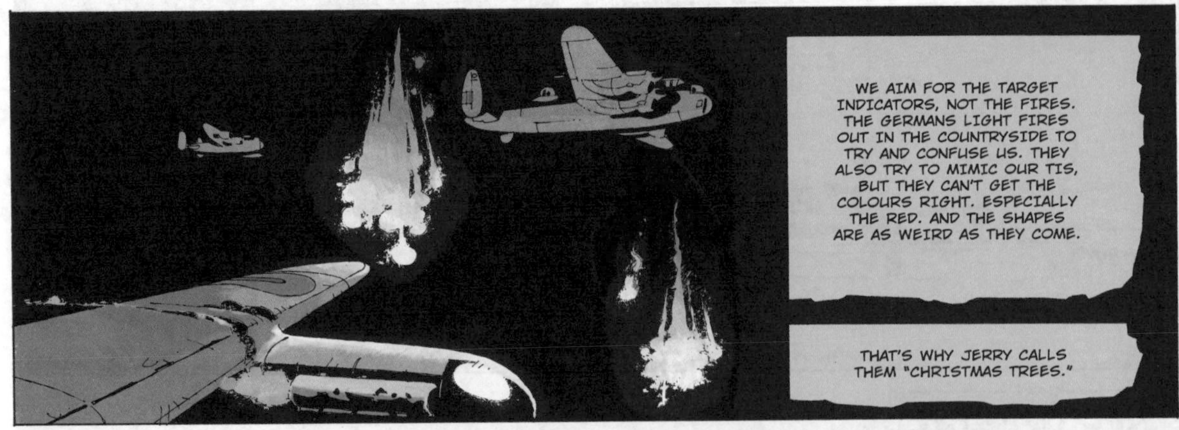
WE AIM FOR THE TARGET INDICATORS, NOT THE FIRES. THE GERMANS LIGHT FIRES OUT IN THE COUNTRYSIDE TO TRY AND CONFUSE US. THEY ALSO TRY TO MIMIC OUR TIS, BUT THEY CAN'T GET THE COLOURS RIGHT. ESPECIALLY THE RED. AND THE SHAPES ARE AS WEIRD AS THEY COME.
THAT'S WHY JERRY CALLS THEM "CHRISTMAS TREES."

ONCE A MAJOR RAID HAS BEGUN, IT QUICKLY REACHES ITS HORRIFYING CLIMAX...
AND ALWAYS THIS SILENCE...

STAND BY, SKIPPER! WE'RE NEARING THE TARGET.
AT THAT POINT, IT'S THE BOMB AIMER WHO CONTROLS THE AIRCRAFT. THE PILOT MERELY FOLLOWS HIS INSTRUCTIONS BLINDLY.

26

FRESH TIS ARE DROPPED REGULARLY. NIGHT RAIDS HAVE A TENDENCY TO "CREEP BACK..."

WHEN A BOMB AIMER DROPS HIS LOAD TOO EARLY AND EVERYBODY USES THE AIRCRAFT BEFORE HIM AS A MARKER...

... YOU END UP BOMBING BRUSSELS INSTEAD OF BERLIN.

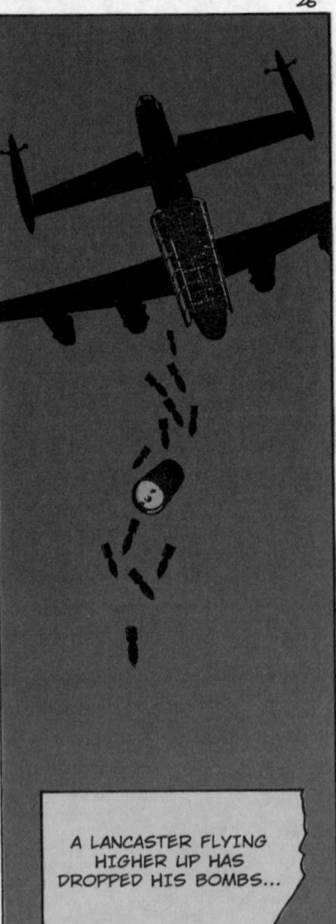
A LANCASTER FLYING HIGHER UP HAS DROPPED HIS BOMBS...

THEY FLUTTER DOWN. SO LIGHT IN APPEARANCE...

... BUT A "COOKIE" WEIGHS TWO TONS. AND SUDDENLY, X-XRAY IS UNDERNEATH...

MAYBE THE MID-UPPER AIR GUNNER SAW THE MONSTER COMING...

OR MAYBE NOT. THE PILOT DIDN'T TRY TO DODGE.

I THINK: IT'D BE LESS CYNICAL OF THE UNIVERSE IF THEY'D BEEN SHOT DOWN BY FLAK, OR A FIGHTER.
AND THEN: HEIGHT IS SAFETY. I FEEL AS MUCH THREATENED FROM ABOVE AS BELOW. BUT I CAN'T CLIMB NOW. I HAVE TO FOLLOW MY BOMB AIMER'S DIRECTIONS...
27
EASY... RIGHT... EEEASY!

DUMMY RUN.
DUMMY R...! OH, THAT DAFT LITTLE TWIT! I TRY NOT TO YELL.
WE DON'T GET TO DO DUMMY RUNS OVER BERLIN, BOMB AIMER. LAY YOUR EGGS!
BUT, SKIPPER...
I CAN'T HOLD IT.
NO BUTS
DROP THE BLOODY BOMB
DURING TRAINING, WHEN YOU CAN'T LOCATE YOUR OBJECTIVE QUITE CLEARLY, YOU CIRCLE AROUND AND HAVE ANOTHER GO. THAT'S WHAT THEY CALL A "DUMMY RUN." AND IT'S ALL NICE AND GOOD IN BROAD DAYLIGHT OVER LINCOLNSHIRE...
... BUT NOT HERE!
NOT HERE!
HEY? WHAT THE...?
OH, SHIT!
BANDIT! BANDIT!
CORKSCREW, SKIPPER! DIVE! HEAVENS, AUBIE, GET US OUT OF HERE!
CORKSCREW. SHARP DIVING TURN TO PORT, FOLLOWED BY A SHARP CLIMBING TURN TO STARBOARD. IT PUTS A HELL OF A STRAIN ON THE PLANE'S AIRFRAME. A BARELY CONTROLLED FREE FALL...
THE ONLY WAY TO SHAKE OFF A NIGHT FIGHTER...
MAY THE BEST CREW SURVIVE.

HE HIT THE TAIL FIN, SKIPPER. THAT WAS CLOSE... SHIT!
BANDIT'S COMING BACK, AUBIE!
THE ROUNDEL ON THE SIDE OF THE LANC MAKES FOR A LOVELY TARGET...
AND BEHIND IT IS ALAN...
WE HEAR HIM SCREAM OVER THE BURST THAT CUTS HIM IN TWO.
29
AN ENGINE'S HIT-PORT INNER. I SHUT IT OFF BEFORE IT CATCHES ON FIRE. IT'S THE ONE THAT CONTROLS THE REAR TURRET'S HYDRAULIC SYSTEM. OUR REAR GUNNER IS SUDDENLY PARALYSED. DEFENCELESS!

THE ONLY BIT OF ARMOUR PLATING IN A LANCASTER PROTECTS THE KITE'S ONE VITAL ELEMENT...
BH S
... THE PILOT'S HEAD! THERE'S NO SECONDARY, NO DUAL CONTROLS...
IF I BUY IT, THEY ALL BUY IT.
COLIN...
YVETTE...
OK, CHAPS. I'VE GOT HER BACK UNDER CONTROL. CREW CHECK. BOMB AIMER?
NO ANSWER.
NAVIGATOR?
OK, AUBIE. ALAN AND COLIN ARE DEAD. THE COMPASS IS ON THE BLINK.

*NICKNAME FOR THE REAR AIR GUNNER

R-ROOO-R-R-ROOO-R-ROOOOO O-

U-UNCLE ON APPROACH. TOWER: I'M OUT OF JUICE.
ROGER, U-UNCLE. CLEAR TO LAND ON RUNWAY TWO.

T-TANGO CHECKING IN. EVERYTHING'S FINE.
ROGER, TANGO. CIRCLE AT 3,000.

A/C LET
CAPTAIN
T F/L COWIE
X F/S JULIAN
S F/S AUBERSON
G F/S LEMIEUX
L F/O VISMARA

L-LOVE CHECKING IN.
Z-ZULU CHECKING IN.
RAF

G-GEORGE CHECKING IN. MAYDAY! MAYDAY! I'VE LOST JUST ABOUT EVERYTHING BUT THE WINGS, CHAPS!
ROGER, GEORGE. YOU'RE CLEAR TO LAND.

IF HE TAKES IT EASY, HE CAN STAY IN THE AIR FOR AT LEAST ANOTHER HOUR AND A HALF. CHIN UP, CORPORAL.

YES, SIR.

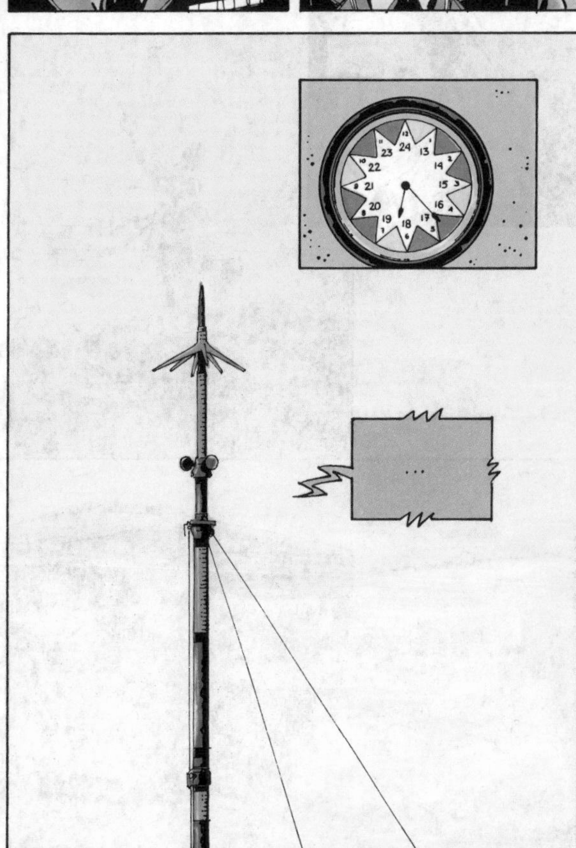
...

NIGEL'S COME BACK TO HIS SENSES AFTER SOME MORE NONSENSE ABOUT HIS SERGEANT MAJOR. HE'S ALL RIGHT NOW. S-SNOWWHITE IS CRABBING ITS WAY BACK TOWARDS THE ENGLISH SHORE.

.AYDAY M..DAY
S-.NOW..ITE TO TOWER... TWO DEAD AND... INJURED... BOARD. REQU... IMM...ATE CLEARANCE TO .AND.

RUN ALONG NOW, PETERS.

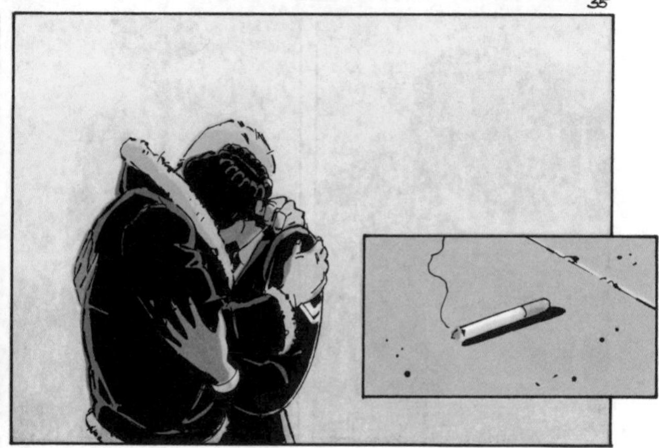

W.A.A.F.
OUT OF BOUNDS
TO R.A.F.
WITHIN 25 FEET
OF THIS NOTICE

HUT 7
W.A.A.F.

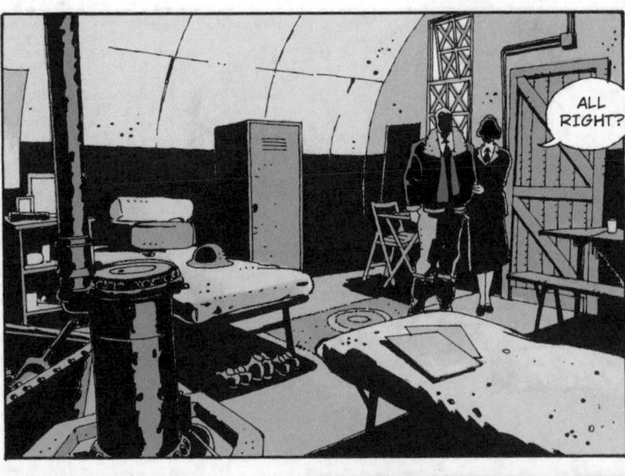
ALL RIGHT?

FAMOUS
LAST
WORDS
AS YOU CAN SEE...

...

TEMPO
THERE'LL BE BLUEBIRDS OVER
THE WHITE CLIFFS OF DOVER
TOMORROW JUST YOU WAIT AND SEE

THERE'LL BE LOVE AND LAUGHTER

AND PEACE EVER AFTER

TOMORROW

WHEN THE WORLD IS FREE

THE SHEPHERD WILL TEND HIS SHEEP

THE VALLEY WILL BLOOM AGAIN

AND JIMMY WILL GO TO SLEEP

IN HIS OWN LITTLE ROOM AGAIN

THERE'LL BE BLUEBIRDS OVER
YOUR NEAREST
AIR RAID SHELTER
IS No 71 REAR OF HUT EIGHT

37

THE WHITE CLIFFS OF DOVER

TOMORROW

JUST YOU WAIT AND SEE

BUT THE WINDOW WAS CLOSED, AND THERE WERE IRON BARS ON IT, AND PEERING INSIDE HE SAW HIS MOTHER SLEEPING PEACEFULLY WITH HER ARM AROUND ANOTHER LITTLE BOY.

PETER CALLED, "MOTHER! MOTHER!" BUT SHE HEARD HIM NOT; IN VAIN HE BEAT HIS LITTLE LIMBS AGAINST THE IRON BARS. HE HAD TO FLY BACK, SOBBING, TO THE GARDENS, AND HE NEVER SAW HIS DEAR MOTHER AGAIN. WHAT A GLORIOUS BOY HE HAD MEANT TO BE TO HER!

AH, PETER! WE WHO HAVE MADE THE GREAT MISTAKE, HOW DIFFERENTLY WE SHOULD ALL ACT AT THE SECOND CHANCE.

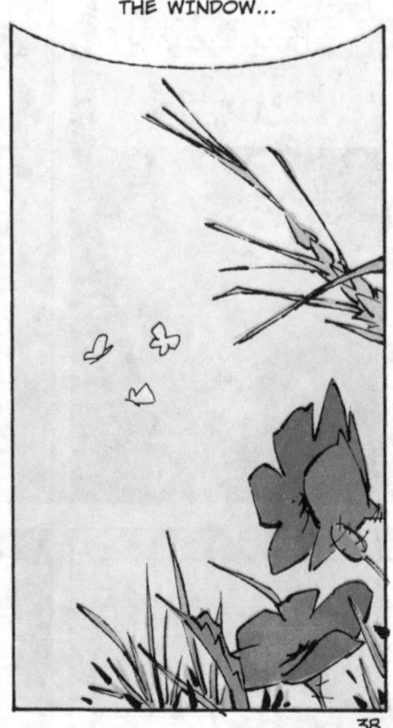
BUT SOLOMON WAS RIGHT—THERE IS NO SECOND CHANCE, NOT FOR MOST OF US. WHEN WE REACH THE WINDOW...

... IT IS LOCK-OUT TIME. THE IRON BARS ARE UP FOR LIFE.
END OF CHAPTER.
THAT WAS LOVELY, LISA. YOU READ VERY WELL.
I KNOW IT ALMOST BY HEART. MUMMY USED TO READ ME PETER PAN STORIES ON OUR WALKS IN KENSINGTON GARDENS. DAVID, WHY DIDN'T YOU BRING YOUR DOLL?
SHE WAS SH... SHE FELL OFF THE PLANE.

THAT'S TOO BAD.

MY DADDY FELL FROM HIS PLANE TOO.

THAT'S WHY HIS LEG STILL HURTS HIM.
!

YOUR DAD WAS A PILOT?
YES. A LONG TIME AGO, WHEN THE GERMANS WERE BOMBING LONDON.

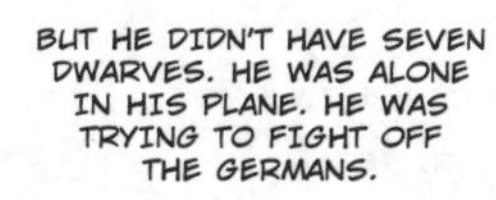
BUT HE DIDN'T HAVE SEVEN DWARVES. HE WAS ALONE IN HIS PLANE. HE WAS TRYING TO FIGHT OFF THE GERMANS.

THEY ALWAYS CAME BACK. MUMMY AND I WERE SCARED, BUT DADDY COULDN'T STAY WITH US. HE HAD TO FIGHT THE GERMAN PLANES.

39

ONE DAY, I WAS WALKING DOWN THE STREET WITH SNOW WHITE AND MUMMY WHEN A BOMB FELL. JUST ONE. REALLY CLOSE.

WE DIDN'T EVEN HEAR THE PLANE. AND THEN... SUDDENLY, EVERYTHING WAS ON FIRE.

MUMMY TOO.

THERE WAS NO AIRCRAFT...
!

... IT WAS A DELAYED ACTION FUSE.

BOMBS LIKE THOSE EXPLODE HOURS, EVEN DAYS, AFTER THE RAID.

THEIR PURPOSE IS TO DISORGANISE RESCUE EFFORTS AS MUCH AS POSSIBLE.

BUT I DON'T NEED TO TELL YOU THIS, FLIGHT SERGEANT. YOU'RE WELL AWARE OF IT.

40

AFTER ALL, YOU TAKE THE SAME TYPE OF BOMBS TO GERMANY.

IS DAVID ANGRY, DAD?
ANGRY? NO, SWEETIE.
NO.

NOT ANGRY.

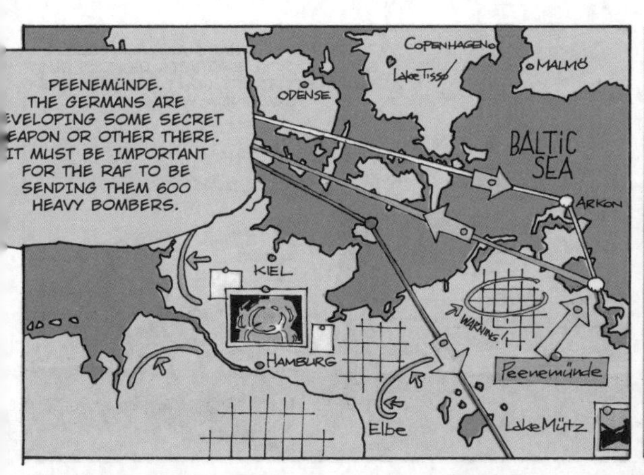
PEENEMÜNDE.
THE GERMANS ARE
EVELOPING SOME SECRET
EAPON OR OTHER THERE.
IT MUST BE IMPORTANT
FOR THE RAF TO BE
SENDING THEM 600
HEAVY BOMBERS.
COPENHAGEN
MALMÖ
Lake Tisso
ODENSE
BALTIC SEA
ARKON
KIEL
HAMBURG
WARNING!
Peenemünde
Elbe
Lake Mütz

S-SNOWWHITE ISN'T
GOING TO PEENEMÜNDE.

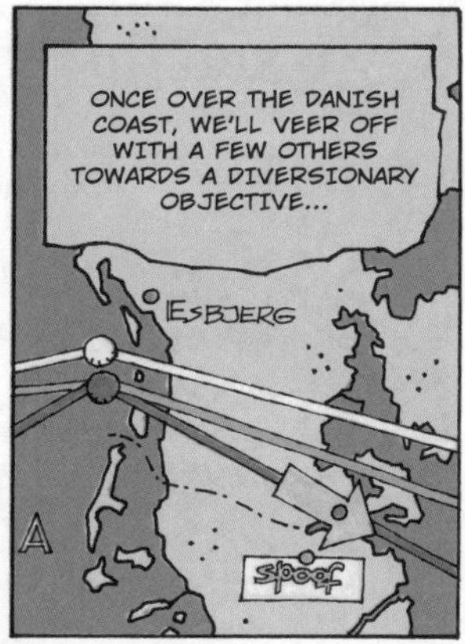
ONCE OVER THE DANISH
COAST, WE'LL VEER OFF
WITH A FEW OTHERS
TOWARDS A DIVERSIONARY
OBJECTIVE...
ESBJERG
spoof

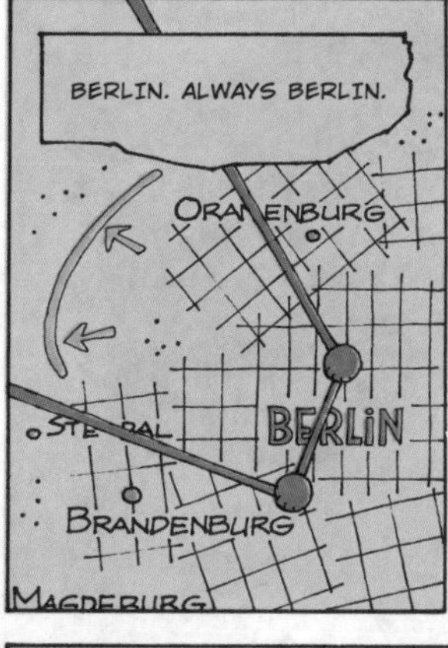
BERLIN. ALWAYS BERLIN.
BERLIN
BRANDENBURG

HEY,
AUBIE! VISITORS
FOR YOU!
SNOWWHITE
!

41

MY DAUGHTER
WOULD LIKE TO TELL
YOU SOMETHING,
FLIGHT SERGEANT.

DAVID, WHO'S PROTECTING YOU NOW THAT YOUR DOLL FELL OFF THE PLANE?

YOU CAN TAKE SNOW WHITE. MAYBE SHE'LL PROTECT YOU THE WAY SHE PROTECTED ME THAT DAY IN LONDON. YOU CAN HAVE HER.

LISA... I... THAT'S AWFULLY NICE. BUT... NO DOLL PROTECTS US. IT'S JUST SUPERSTITION. I DON'T WANT TO TAKE YOUR SNOW WHITE. I...
FLIGHT.

THANK YOU, LISA. I'LL LOOK AFTER HER. AND I'LL GIVE HER BACK TO YOU.

I PROMISE.

GOOD LUCK FLIGHT.

42

LET'S GO, AUBIE. THE CHAP WITH THE LITTLE MOUSTACHE IS WAITING FOR US IN BERLIN.

BESIDES, THE LASS IS MUCH TOO YOUNG FOR YOU!
YEAH, AUBIE. YOU COULD BE HER FATHER!
OH, SHUT UP, YOU TWITS.

THE FREYA RADAR DETECTS THE ENEMY FROM A LONG WAY AWAY.
THEN THE SHORTER-RANGE WÜRZBURG TAKES OVER.
IT'S BETTER ABLE TO DIVINE OUR NUMBERS, OUR ALTITUDE AND OUR HEADING...
43
A SECOND WÜRZBURG GUIDES THE GERMAN FIGHTERS TOWARDS THEIR TARGETS...

*A GERMAN CONCEPT ROUGHLY MEANING HOMELAND, AND A PERSON'S LOVE AND ATTACHMENT TO IT

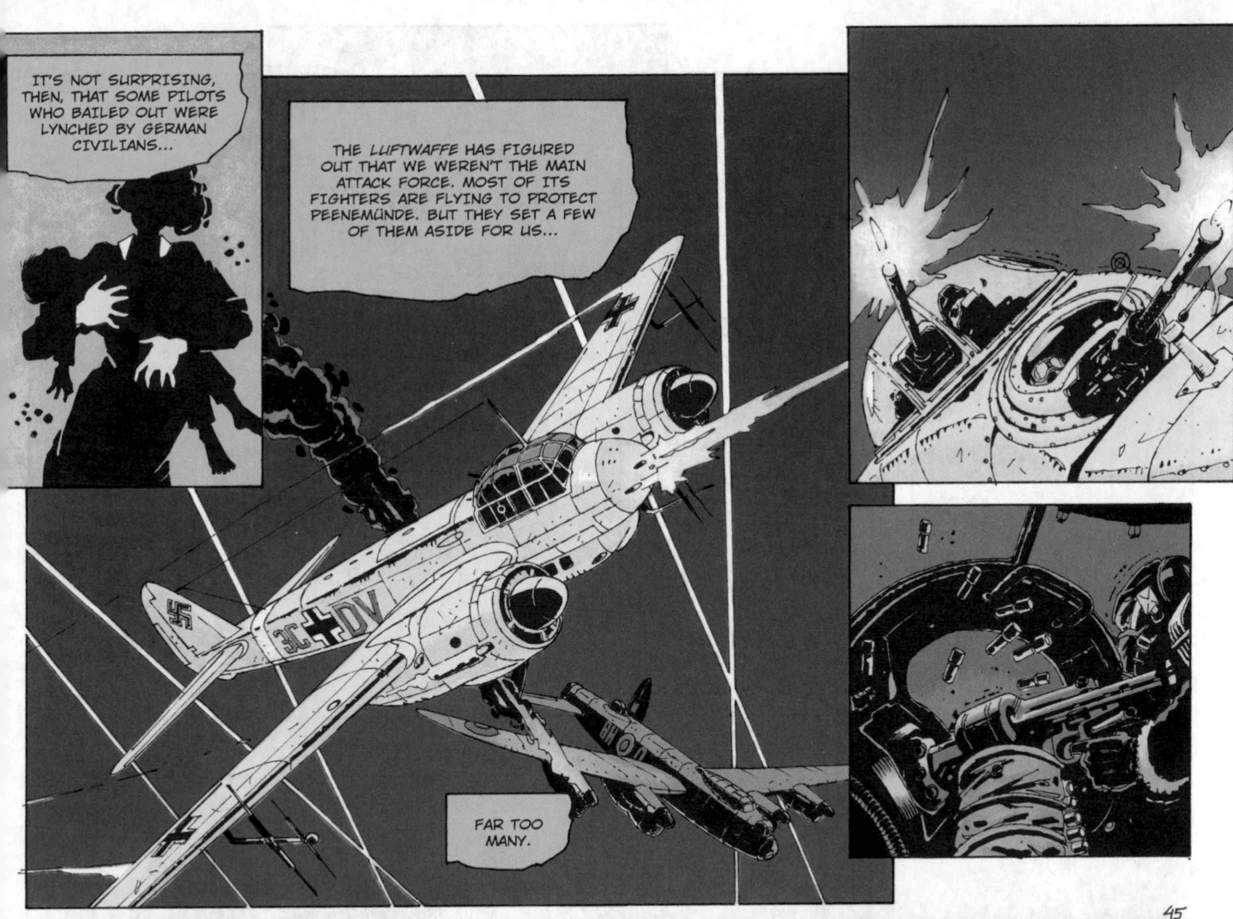
IT'S NOT SURPRISING, THEN, THAT SOME PILOTS WHO BAILED OUT WERE LYNCHED BY GERMAN CIVILIANS...
THE *LUFTWAFFE* HAS FIGURED OUT THAT WE WEREN'T THE MAIN ATTACK FORCE. MOST OF ITS FIGHTERS ARE FLYING TO PROTECT PEENEMÜNDE. BUT THEY SET A FEW OF THEM ASIDE FOR US...
FAR TOO MANY.

SOMEHOW, THOUGH, SNOW WHITE SEEMS TO BE BRINGING S-SNOWWHITE GOOD LUCK... WE AVOID THE SEARCHLIGHTS...

THE FLAK IS NOWHERE NEAR. WELL, NOWHERE NEAR US...

SMOKING IS FORBIDDEN ON BOARD. BUT, SOMETIMES, WHEN EVERYTHING HAS GONE WELL AND WE'RE FLYING LOW ENOUGH FOR ME TO TAKE OFF MY OXYGEN MASK, I ALLOW MYSELF THE PLEASURE OF A CIGARETTE DURING THE FLIGHT HOME.
SORRY, SARAH.

WHEN I DO, THE ENGINEER AND I HAVE THIS IMMUTABLE RITUAL...
TONY, DO YOU SMELL PETROL?
...
AUBIE, PUT OUT THAT BLOODY FAG! YOU JUST SAID YOU SMELLED PETROL!
NEGATIVE. I WAS ASKING YOU IF YOU SMELLED PETROL.
46
AND IT WAS THAT NIGHT...
... THAT S-SNOWWHITE DIDN'T COME BACK. I KNOW.

WERE YOU WAITING FOR HIM, TOO?
YES. IT WAS RAINING... I WAITED, WAITED... I REMEMBER THAT WHEN MY FATHER CAME TO GET ME, I WAS DRENCHED.
AND YOU?

I WAS ON DUTY.

SO, THIS WAS S-SNOWWHITE'S SPOT?
YES.

THIS IS WHERE YOU GAVE HIM YOUR DOLL, ON THAT EVENING OF AUGUST 17, 1943. CONSIDER IT AN OLD WOMAN'S SENTIMENTAL WHIM...

... TO RETURN IT TO YOU ON THAT SAME SPOT.

47

BUT WHY ONLY NOW? WHY 50 YEARS LATER?
I DIDN'T KNOW THIS DOLL BELONGED TO YOU. IT ALL BEGAN WITH A MISUNDER-STANDING.

YOU MUST HAVE GATHERED FROM HIS LETTER THAT OUR RELATIONSHIP WAS SHORT. BACK THEN, YOU KNOW... WAR WAS TEACHING US TO TAKE LIFE ONE DAY AT A TIME. EVERY DAY WAS A UNIQUE MOMENT. THE MOST WE HOPED FOR WAS THAT IT'D LAST UNTIL THE NIGHT, AND TOMORROW WOULD BE A NEW DAY IF IT CAME.

WE BARELY KNEW EACH OTHER. IN TRUTH, WE WERE KEEPING SO MANY SECRETS.

HE'D TOLD ME ABOUT YVETTE, S-SNOWWHITE'S MASCOT, BUT I'D NEVER SEEN HER. AND HE NEVER TALKED TO ME AGAIN ABOUT THAT RAID ON BERLIN, ON THAT NIGHT THEY LOST COLIN AND ALAN. AND YVETTE–ALTHOUGH I ONLY JUST LEARNT THAT PART.
BUT... I DON'T UNDERSTAND NOW...

IN 1946, I WAS VISITED BY ONE MARIJKE DE VRIES, A DUTCHWOMAN WHOSE PARENTS HAD BEEN IN THE RESISTANCE. SHE TOLD ME ABOUT A BOMBER SHOT DOWN OVER THE NETHERLANDS DURING THE NIGHT OF THE 17TH TO THE 18TH OF AUGUST, 1943. HER PARENTS HID THE PILOT, WHO'D BROKEN HIS ANKLE IN THE JUMP. HE HAD A DOLL. YOUR DOLL. SNOW WHITE.

HE ONLY KNEW YOUR FIRST NAME, LISA. JUST YOUR FIRST NAME. I WAS EASIER TO LOCATE. SO HE ASKED HIS HOSTS TO RETURN THE DOLL TO **ME** IN CASE SOMETHING HAPPENED. AFTER THAT, ALL I HAVE...
48
... ARE SPECULATIONS. I SUPPOSE AUBIE WOULD HAVE WANTED TO ADD A SPOKEN MESSAGE, BUT A FEW DAYS LATER, HE WAS ARRESTED BY THE *GESTAPO* ALONG WITH MARIJKE'S PARENTS. AND NONE OF THEM EVER CAME BACK...

MARIJKE FULFILLED HIS WISH WHEN SHE BROUGHT ME THE DOLL AFTER THE WAR.

AND I'VE LIVED THE PAST 50 YEARS IN THE BELIEF THAT, FROM BEYOND THE GRAVE, AUBIE HAD GIVEN ME S-SNOWWHITE'S MASCOT AS A FAREWELL.

MRS PETERS...
AUBERSON.
?
MRS AUBERSON, I STILL DON'T UNDERSTAND. WHAT ABOUT THE LETTER? WHERE DID IT COME FROM? AND WHAT DID YOU MEAN BY "A SPOKEN MESSAGE"?

THE LETTER... LET'S START WITH THE LETTER.

COULD YOU SHOW LISA THE ARTICLE? ESPECIALLY THE PHOTOGRAPHS?...

HEAVENS!... S-SNOWWHITE...
National Geographic, April 1993
"ONE OF OUR BOMBERS IS NO LONGER MISSING!"
BY PET

THE WRECK WAS RECENTLY FOUND INSIDE A DUTCH POLDER THAT WAS BEING DRAINED...

49

NIGEL'S REMAINS WERE STILL INSIDE THE REAR TURRET. HE HADN'T DROWNED. HE'D BEEN SHOT IN THE AIR. AS FOR THE OTHERS, THE AIRCRAFT WAS EMPTY.

SHOW HER THE OTHER PHOTOGRAPH, DAVID.
!

DAVID... OF COURSE... YOU LOOK LIKE YOUR FATHER.
THANK YOU.

THAT'S WHAT MY MOTHER SAYS.

THIS PICTURE WAS TAKEN BEFORE THE RAID ON BERLIN, SINCE COLIN AND ALAN ARE IN IT...

I'M SORRY. I STILL DON'T SEE WHAT YOU'RE GETTING AT...

LOOK AT WHAT ALBIE'S GOT IN HIS HANDS.

CAN YOU IMAGINE WHAT I FELT WHEN I REALISED THAT THE DOLL THAT HAD BEEN ON MY NIGHT TABLE FOR NEARLY 50 YEARS, NEXT TO HIS PICTURE, WAS **NOT** YVETTE?

I PICKED UP THE DOLL, TURNED IT OVER IN MY HANDS. I DIDN'T UNDERSTAND ANYMORE.

AND SUDDENLY, I SAW THEM. I RECOGNISED THEM.

THE STITCHES THAT **HE**'D SEWN.

I UNDID THEM AND FOUND THE LETTER. THE ONLY LETTER HE EVER WROTE TO ME...
... NOW, 50 YEARS LATER, IT'S AS MUCH FOR YOU AS IT IS FOR ME...

I IMAGINE HE SEWED THE LETTER INSIDE THE DOLL TO MAKE SURE THEY WOULDN'T BE SEPARATED...

I IMAGINE THAT IT WAS THE SPOKEN MESSAGE I SHOULD HAVE RECEIVED—THAT THERE WAS A LETTER **INSIDE** THE DOLL...

A LETTER IN WHICH HE ASKED ME TO RETURN HER DOLL TO THE LITTLE GIRL WHO LIVED ON THE FARM.

IT TOOK US THREE MONTHS TO LOCATE YOU, ELISABETH OWEN...

DAUGHTER OF WING COMMANDER JOSEPH "JOE" OWEN, WHO LOST HIS WIFE IN THE BLITZ AND WAS HIMSELF BADLY INJURED WHEN HIS SPITFIRE WAS SHOT DOWN DURING THE BATTLE OF BRITAIN...

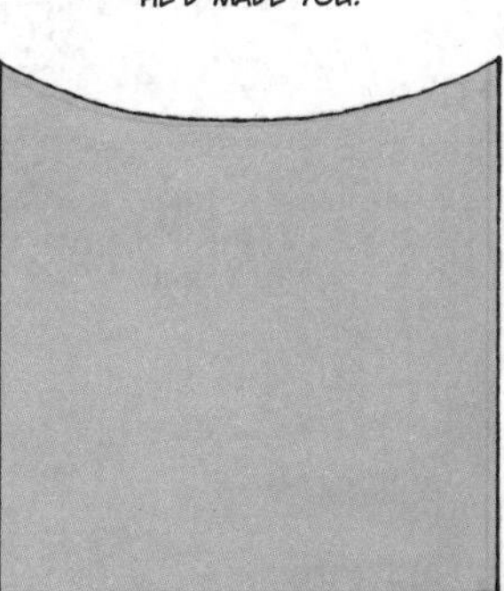
IT TOOK HALF A CENTURY FOR AUBIE TO KEEP THE PROMISE HE'D MADE YOU.

IT'S STRANGE TO READ HERE, IN THE VERY PLACE WHERE HE TOOK OFF FOR THE LAST TIME, THIS LETTER IN WHICH HE TELLS YOU... US... WHY HE RISKED HIS LIFE NIGHT AFTER NIGHT...
YES, WHY?
51

READ THE LAST LINE OF HIS LETTER, LISA.

52

COLOURS:
CLAUDE LEGRIS

MARVANO 29/6/92